Your Plans for Writing a Book
Practical Tools for Helping Writers Outline
Novels, Stories, Screenplays, Memoirs, Nonfiction and Self-Help Books
from Start to Finish

Buddha Press

For information on discounts for bulk purchases please contact info@buddhapress.com
To find other books by this author please go to www.kathrinlake.com
Printed in United States and Canada
ISBN: 978 1503 391857

Your Plans

for

Writing a Book

Practical Tools for Helping Writers
Outline Novels, Stories, Screenplays,
Memoirs, Nonfiction and Self-Help Books
from Start to Finish

Kathrin Lake

Table of Contents

Introduction

I have to confess that I dislike introductions. It is like forcing hungry kids at the dinner table to wait through someone's dull speech. I am a jump-into-the-meat-of-the-book kind of reader when it comes to how-to books. That said, there are some distinctions I would like to give about this workbook – and this is what this book is, a workbook with some explanation and a lot of tools. These tools have grown out of decades of teaching and coaching writing skills that have crossed all kinds of genres. And in those years, I found that the biggest struggle for writers is structuring and outlining long-form works successfully. That means novels, plays, screenplays, memoirs and non-fiction books. So I have notes here for **Fiction Writers and Nonfiction Writers...**

Fiction Writers

I realize that the title of this manual indicates it is for writing books and for fiction that mean novels, yet plays and screenplays are clearly not books. It may surprise you to learn that the best tools within - which are relevant for all fiction writers - I found from trying to write or adapt stories for the screen or stage. Using screenplay techniques to outline a novel was tremendously helpful to the struggling novelists I was working with. I have now borrowed a lot of screenwriting and even actors' techniques that I found really worked for character and story development which virtually all fiction writers can use. You will also notice that this manual starts with character versus story because all stories should flow from characters and not the other way around. But what does all this have to do with non-fiction writers?

Non-Fiction Writers

As much as I love helping others write fiction, the majority of my clients are writing non-fiction books by about a 60% to 40% ratio. But the non-fiction writer cannot and should not ignore story or story form. After studying many successful non-fiction books, you will notice that they always include stories or case studies as a basis for getting their points across. Psychologically, our best communication tool is not to tell people things flatly, but put it in the context of a story, and if the story is "true," so much the better. Think of one of the most successful non-fiction book series, Chicken Soup for the Soul (there are over 250 versions), which are comprised only of "true" stories.

You may have noticed that I put quotation marks around the word "true" when referencing true stories (non-fiction), and that is because all true stories are interpretations of the truth. You can include the basic facts as true, but what really happened in detail is subjective and rarely provable to a finite degree. That is where memoirists and non-fiction writers need to know story structure and how to create imagined details to create a better story. They too can learn from the fiction advice and tools here. Not to worry, I also have a great respect for journalistic ethics and how to create non-fiction books that are as factual as they are engaging. To that end, I have provided my non-fiction writers and memoirists with all the tools they will need for structuring their successful non-fiction books.

There you have it. The dreaded introduction is over, and you can dig in. Bon appetite!

Kathrin Lake

PS - This book was designed to be written in, but any of the graphs can be easily converted into spreadsheets if you prefer to do that. Personally, I find it easier to be at my computer with my manuscript, and consult my hand written plotting book versus switching screens. Whatever way you do it, the basic ideas and explanations for plotting are what you will gain from, and will be able to use as a reference for any project.

FOR *Fiction Writers*

Novels, plays, screenplays,
(and storytellers in nonfiction)

FICTION WRITERS
8 Essential Things the Fiction Writer Must Learn
(again and again)

1. Writers Rewrite
The famous response by Truman Capote when a writer claimed he never rewrote his work was, "That's not writing, that's typing," says it all. Get comfortable with the fact that even when you think you're finished, you rarely are. Anne Lamott says we all write "shitty first drafts." Then we rewrite. And rewrite some more.

2. Show Don't Tell
If you can only remember one piece of writing advice, "show don't tell" is the one. Exposition, explaining or telling a story, whether it is through the narrator or through the character's thoughts, can quickly lead to dull, flat writing. If you keep your story in the present, and very active, you engage and grip a reader. Showing what the characters are doing - action - and therefore their intentions, is much stronger. It will often prevent a writer from overwriting. Writers need to show what is happening and stay with the story - far less tangents. (See the Checklist for Fiction Writers).

3. Write What You Know and Research the Rest
It is an old adage, but writing what you know simply means that you already have your in-depth research in the bank. If you write about something you don't know, and start on a potentially long path of research, beware you don't get lost there. This is a good argument for writing not only about what you know, but what you read. Read all the best in the genre you are writing in, and then write from your own place of knowledge, and your own imagination of possibilities. At some point you will have to do fact checking, often on the fly, but it helps to know your genre and your research well. If research isn't your strong suit, then, go with that old adage and write what you already know, as long as you are excited about it.

4. Read it Out Loud - Dialogue

All writing can be tested for flow by reading it out loud. I learned this in the theatre. AND, it is absolutely essential that all dialogue be tested this way. In conversations, we speak to people in clipped phrases that follow the context of a conversation within its setting. A writer can only understand what works in her dialogue by reading it aloud as if she was in that context and that setting. She should also test this using the literal voice of that character. So, if a writer says their character has a southern drawl, then they must speak the characters dialogue aloud in that imagined southern drawl to test it. This will also help a writer better connect to their characters, as well as reduce a writer's wordiness. Most writers tend to overwrite their dialogue, and reading aloud will show you where to cut.

5. Know Your Story Structure

Story structure hinges on what characters want, and what their overarching purpose is for the duration of the story. It is only by knowing that, that the writer can create the obstacles in the characters paths and figure out how they will resolve them. This is your story structure. Understanding it and improving on it is your job as a storyteller. To that end much of the tools in this manual are focused on story structure.

6. Raising the Stakes

Part of the improvement of a story structure is by "raising the stakes" for your characters. In translation, that means make it harder and worse for them. You can do this by simply making a piece of bad news the character receives come at the worst possible time, in the worst possible location. Or, just when the character has started to win a gamble, you have to force them to risk even more. When they are madly in love, they find out their object of desire is married or otherwise unobtainable. This is raising the stakes.

7. Plausibility

Not all of what you write will be based on real facts, much won't, but it will have to be plausible. In the internet age of instant answers this is more relevant than ever, but it has always been so. The devil is in the details when it comes to plausibility. Elements of fiction should feel true even if they aren't true. We call this "suspension of disbelief." If you craft your story elements with a good base of not exact but "similar" truths, or some cold hard research, or just a commitment to a more plausible fantasy, then even skeptics will forgive you, and readers will love your stories.

8. Let the Character and Work Lead, Not Your Ego

I caution new writers about creating characters (and thereby stories), that represent their own ego ideals. Perfection kills. Be brave enough to let your characters do things you would never want to do and say things that would make you cringe and blush. Create compelling characters. Characters really are like your children and if you let them, they will rebel against you. This is good, and you need to resist the urge to control them. Be instead, a good detective. Look at why a character might act the way they do, what is their intention? Let the characters and the work lead. Not wanting to be a likable writer who creates likeable characters is essential. For more on how characters lead, read *Writing with Cold Feet*, Chapter 3, "Characters and the Evil Puppet Master" and other things about character.

Back Story & Fleshed Out Characters
How to Use a Character Form (on following pages)

The following **Character Form** is a way to create a character that is fully fleshed out and not flat. It also includes elements for you to create back story. Back story is the character's life, and therefore their psychological make-up, before we ever meet them in your narrative. The deeper you go, the better the character, the better the writing. The elements that I have found the most valuable are in bold and I need to explain them here.

Key Phrase - A Key Phrase is a phrase the character says that unlocks something about their character, because it is true or sometimes the character wants it to be true but its not true. An example is Rick in *Casablanca*, who declares early on in the film that he will not stick his neck out for anybody. We find out in a flashback that it was not always true about him, and how he became cynical. The story then hinges on him meeting the one person in the world who he will stick his neck out for, way out. Therefore this is a key phrase.

Habitual or Favorite Phrase - This is the phrase that is associated with this character such as "Elementary, my dear Watson," (Sherlock Holmes). Or, "I wont' think of that today, I'll think of that tomorrow" (Scarlett O'Hara). Or, "The little gray cells," (Hercule Poirot). This not only gives color to your character but it also reveals something essential about them.

Dread Death - This is the death that the character is most afraid of for themselves. Again, it can add color to the character if it comes up in the narrative, but it can also reveal something important about them. We see Indiana Jones hates snakes early in the film, this could have come up as his Dread Death - death by snakes, and does add color. Another example was when I got to know one character better when I found out that the way he was most afraid of dying was to have a heart attack in public. I suddenly had an insight of how important it was for him to maintain an aura of strength publicly.

Musical Instruments (they play or would play) - Your character may not play a musical instrument, but just thinking about them playing one gives you a deeper emotional feel for this character. Let them be vulnerable here, or brilliant, or funny, or sad. What kind of instrument would they play if they could? I once met a man who wanted to learn the cello so he could put his arms around something.

Other elements in the back story section like happiest time, time they most regret, etc., are for you to write a story or scene as part of their back story. Back stories may or may not come up directly in your fictional narrative, but they do give you a deep sense of the characters internal struggles and motivations.

How do I recommend you get the authentic goods on your character?

Interview them. Don't force it. Close your eyes and ask them.

Character Form

Character name:_____ Name Meaning:_____

Age: _____ Sex: _____ Height: _____ Weight: _____ Eyesight: _____

Hearing: _____ Sexual Orientation: _____

Relationship status:_____ Smoker / Non

Racial Background _____ Grew up: _____

Religious Background_____ Now: _____

Profession:_____ Politics:_____

Hobbies: _____

Birthdate: _____Astrological Sign: _____

Significance of Sign: _____

Automobile/transportation: _____

Pets owned:_____

Scars, Limps, Physical Flaws, etc.: _____

An animal that in appearance, movement, manner, etc. seems like your character? _____

What is it about that animal that relates to your character (be specific)? _____

Is there anyone close to you, family or friend, who is like your character? A famous person? _____

How physically active is your character? _____

Vocally is your character, loud or quiet, gentle or rough, or some other description?_____

Accents?_____ Vocabulary? _____

Usual Facial expression? _____

How does your character dress? Sloppy, neat, fashionable, colorful, radical, conservative, frumpy, tight fitting, loose fitting, jewelry?

_____

_____

How do they wear or comb their hair? Short/Long? Bald? Color? Is it dyed? _____

Their key, habitual or favorite phrase? _____

_____

Their habitual gesture? _____

Character Form - Back Story Section

Write some of these aspects of your main characters' life that tells you something about them. Write at least three of these in scenes (later), where you do your writing (you may or may not use them in your story). Below just write the notes.

Make a Note, then circle 3 to write a scene

1. Their greatest personal weakness _____
2. Their greatest personal strength _____
3. Last or current profession, career, job. _____
4. Ideal living space _____
5. Actual living space _____
6. Lock / Security on their home _____
7. Dread death _____
8. Actual death (if applicable) _____
9. Fantasy of fame _____
10. Favorite snapshot of themselves _____
11. Most hated snapshot of themselves _____
12. Musical instrument they play (or would play) _____
13. Their weapon real, symbolic or something abstract i.e.: their sexuality _____
14. Their shield, (similar to weapon) _____
15. Regrets in life _____
16. Most: Happy moment _____
17. Most Sad moment _____
18. Most Angry moment _____
19. Most Humiliated or vulnerable moment _____
20. Most Afraid _____

Fast Character Graph

Characters	Age	Profession	Strength	Flaw	Habitual Phrase
Example: Jane Doe	16	Part-time Wal-Mart	Takes no crap	Goes too far	No shit Sherlock!

Character Archetypes

There are many character archetypes we can see used again and again in stories. The character plays a role in the story and either helps or hinders the main characters, and sometimes they do both. Your protagonist will also be playing an archetypal role, typically the hero or heroine, but can be a anti-hero, and other roles. Any character can be more than one kind of archetype but they usually have one dominant role in the story.

Monster	Villain	
Outsider	Witch	
Temptress/Femme Fatale	Wizard	*Some to get*
Caretaker/Mother	Robot	*you started.*
Hermit	Alien	*You will be*
Conformist	Crazy person	*able to*
Pillar of Community	Optimist	*discover*
Crazy Genius	Pessimist	*more*
Loner	Intellectual	
Magician	Snob	
Healer	Artist	
Bon Vivant	Exile / Outcast	
Spoiled Brat	Matchmaker	
Gossip	The Romantic	
Religious Zealot	Stubborn One	
Defender	Fixer	
Judge	Polly Anna	
Adult Child	Naughty Child	
Charming Scoundrel	Good Child	
Martyr	Evil Child	
Master Planner	Bully	
Anti-Hero	Miser	
Wise Mentor	Belle	
Rebel	Golden Boy / Girl	
Friend	Celebrity	
Underdog	Loyal Servant	
Innocent / Fool	Sidekick	
Clown	Tortured Soul	
Lover	Slave	

Characters	Archetype Role in Story	BACK STORY: Turning point Incident	Action Result
Example: Jane	Heroine	Emotionally hurt by a man	Never dates
	Hero		
	Mentor		
	Antagonist/ Villain		
	Helper/Friend		

Characters & Theme

Possible Themes - Brainstorm and choose two themes that are dominant in your storyline. **Some Universal Themes:**

Revenge	Dreams	Nature	Trust	Google more
Happiness	Responsibility	Friendship	Love	or add
Control	Humility	Betrayal	Truth	your own!
Power	Faith	Justice	Death	
Survival	Fear	Innocence	Ethics	
Family	Teamwork	Humor	Illusions	
Good vs. Evil	Patriotism	Struggle	Deception	
Spirituality	Community	Inhumanity	Heroism	
Humanity	Communication			

THEMES:		

Main Characters	Relationship to Protagonist	How they feel about Theme 1	How they feel about Theme 2	What are the opposites of theme 1 and 2?

Notes

Write some notes of what you discovered in previous worksheets

Story Structure

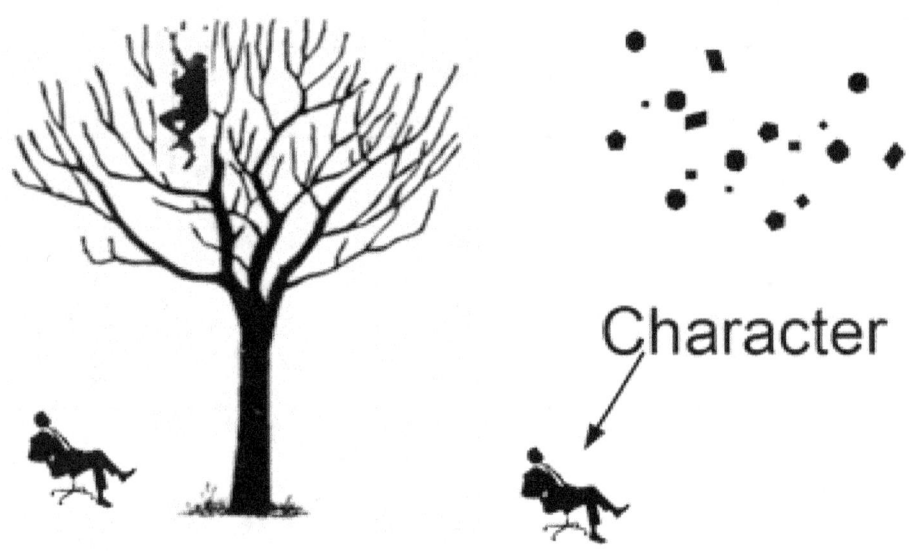

Character

Get your character up a tree, throw rocks at them, get them out of the tree

When is your character up a tree? _____

_____HINT: early on

What is the first rock? _____

_____

What are all the other rocks?

_____

_____

_____

_____

_____

_____

What is the help or solution?

_____

_____

_____

_____

What is the climax - worst point before it gets better?

_____

_____

Is there a second worst point before it gets all the way better?

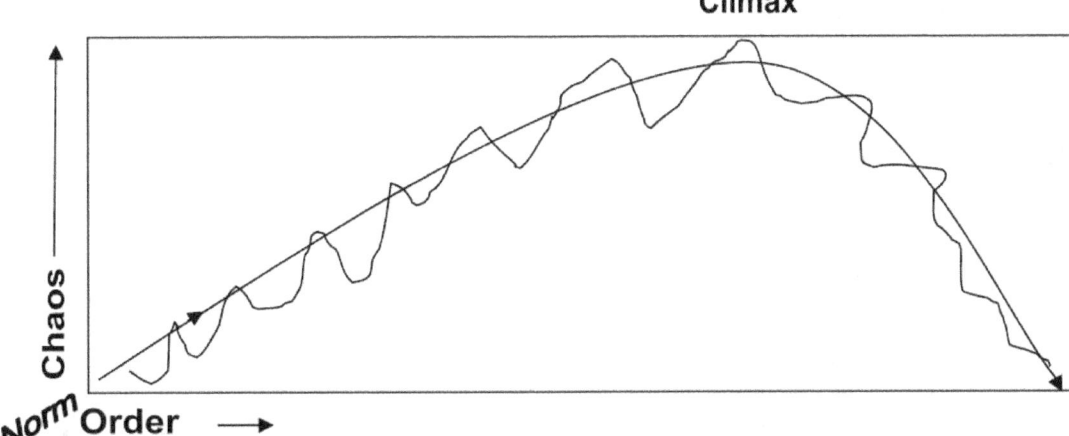

The journey generally starts with a sort of order or **norm** - sometimes the norm is chaos - but it gets to either more chaos or a series of challenges between the main character and the **object of desire**. It is a rocky road, always with ups and downs that include the **rocks** and the **help**. In the end will she get what she desires? Change the desire? The main character will always learn something in the pursuit.

Set-Up - The Norm

Girl dreams of romance; watches movies and reads romance novels. She is going to have a better marriage than her mother who she blames for driving her father away. Girl wants a fairytale wedding and this is her **object of desire.** Girl meets Boy, who woos her, very romantic. She falls in love with him. All seems **normal.**

Example of Rocks and Help - The Rocky Road

🪨 Girl has red flag boy is abusive but ignores it
♥ *Boy and Girl get engaged*
🪨 Girl has next big flag against boy
🪨 Girl is covering up, lying to herself & others
   Girl and Boy get married, wedding is image
🪨 Girl is abused but forgives, denial
🪨 Girl thinks she is going crazy - gaslighted
♥ Girl leaves boy with some help from friend
🪨 Boy wins girl back
🪨 Girl is living an image again
♥ *Boy and Girl have child*
🪨 Girl is isolated with child, covering up abuse
🪨 Girl finds Boy cheating conclusively
♥ Girl confesses all to a friend, gets therapy
🪨 Girl must hide therapy from husband

♥ *Girl begins to remember things from childhood and confirms from her mother that her father was an abuser. Mother hid it, just as she did. Her pursuit changes. Escape.*

🪨 Boy suspects Girl may leave, abuses her
♥ Girl takes kid and escapes
🪨 Boy goes after her to control her
🪨 Boy is friends with a cop and gaslighting him
🪨 Last power struggle, with violence
🪨 Girl is charged w assault, child taken
♥ Help from lawyer, therapist, friend, mother
♥ Truth comes out Girl triumphs in court

Story from Character Motivation

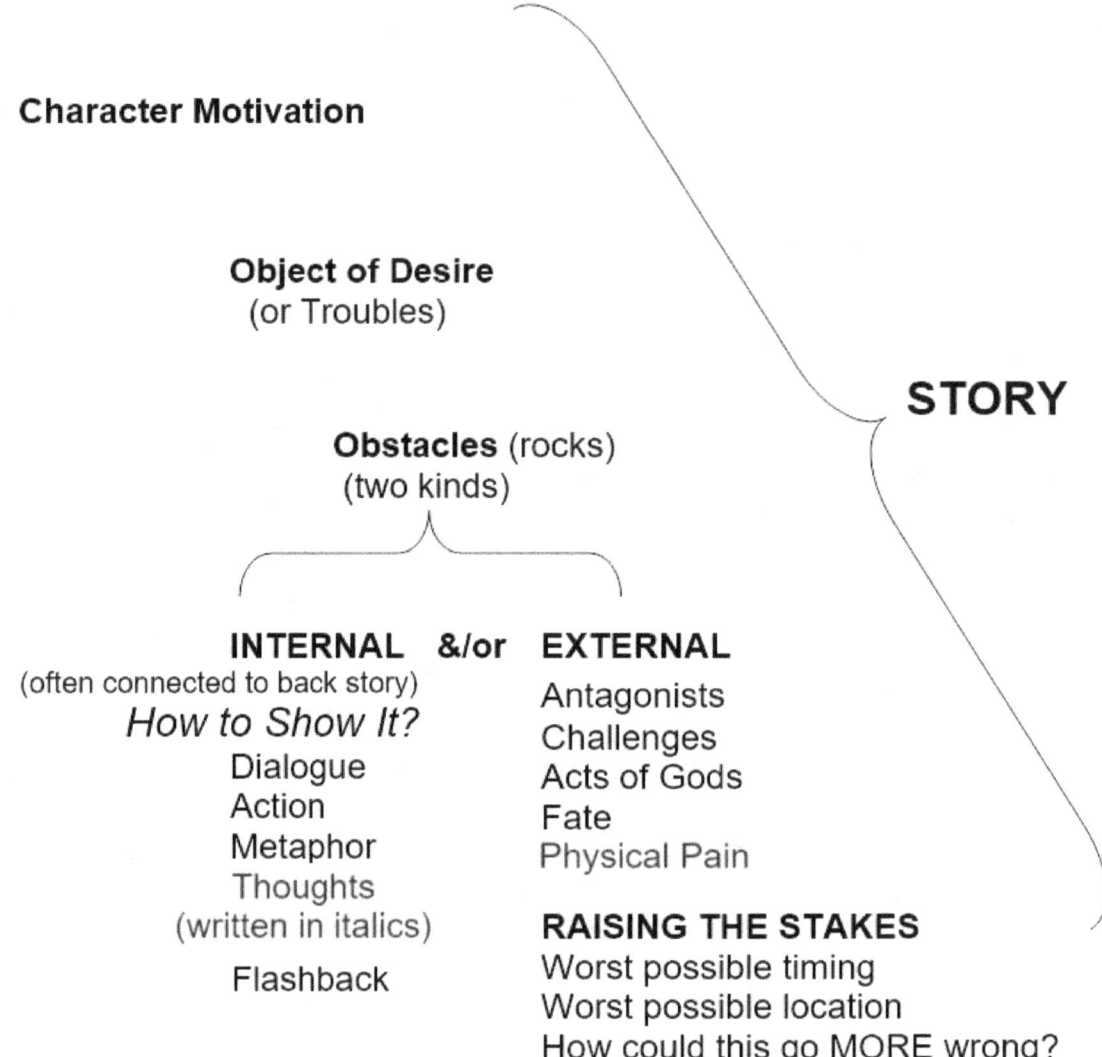

Character Motivation

Object of Desire
(or Troubles)

Obstacles (rocks)
(two kinds)

STORY

INTERNAL **&/or** **EXTERNAL**
(often connected to back story)
How to Show It?
Dialogue
Action
Metaphor
Thoughts
(written in italics)

Flashback

Antagonists
Challenges
Acts of Gods
Fate
Physical Pain

RAISING THE STAKES
Worst possible timing
Worst possible location
How could this go MORE wrong?

Examples of Internal and External Obstacles (rocks)

INTERNAL
Low self esteem
Under a delusion
Belief system block
Not skilled... yet
Past trauma
Innocence
Pessimism

EXTERNAL
Rival
Bureaucracy
Physical obstacle - a mountain, a journey
Not skilled... yet, training to do
Family duties to do
No money
Crisis - weather

Characters' Desire Chart - Example

Example is from one of my own works. Note all major characters have a desire and a fear and sometimes more than one.

Character	Desire 1	Connected Fear	Desire 2	Connected Fear
Brian	Keeping custody of daughter	He will drink and screw it up	Excitement	Choosing the wrong woman, she will leave him for another guy.
Robert	To retire happily	He won't have enough $		
Carrie	To be safe	She will be taken (back story of human trafficked)	Help women	She will be taken again - imprisoned
Mother	To keep Carrie safe	That C will never be happy or normal again	To continue thriving with dogs, training them	Bad people use their guard dogs in bad ways
Twin 1	Thriving biz Money and rich clientele	Economy	Live like the rich clients they service	Time is running out
Twin 2	Ethical business	His bro will get him into trouble - liabilities		
Police woman	To be respected – a big bust	It will never be enough		

Characters' Desire Chart - Blank

Character	Desire 1	Connected Fear	Desire 2	Connected Fear

Characters' Desire Chart - Blank

Character	Desire 1	Connected Fear	Desire 2	Connected Fear

Characters' Obstacles - Blank

Figure out major obstacles in advance. They may change but put the ones you know.

Character & Desire 1	Obstacle 1	Obstacle 2	Obstacle 3	Obstacle 4	Obstacle 5

Characters' Obstacles - Blank

Character & Desire 2	Obstacle 1	Obstacle 2	Obstacle 3	Obstacle 4	Obstacle 5

Relationship Triangle

This triangle represents one way of looking at ALL character's relationships within a story. The simplest form has only one outer antagonist, and more than one helper to the protagonist or main character. Antagonists are obstacles to the character's desire, in the flesh.

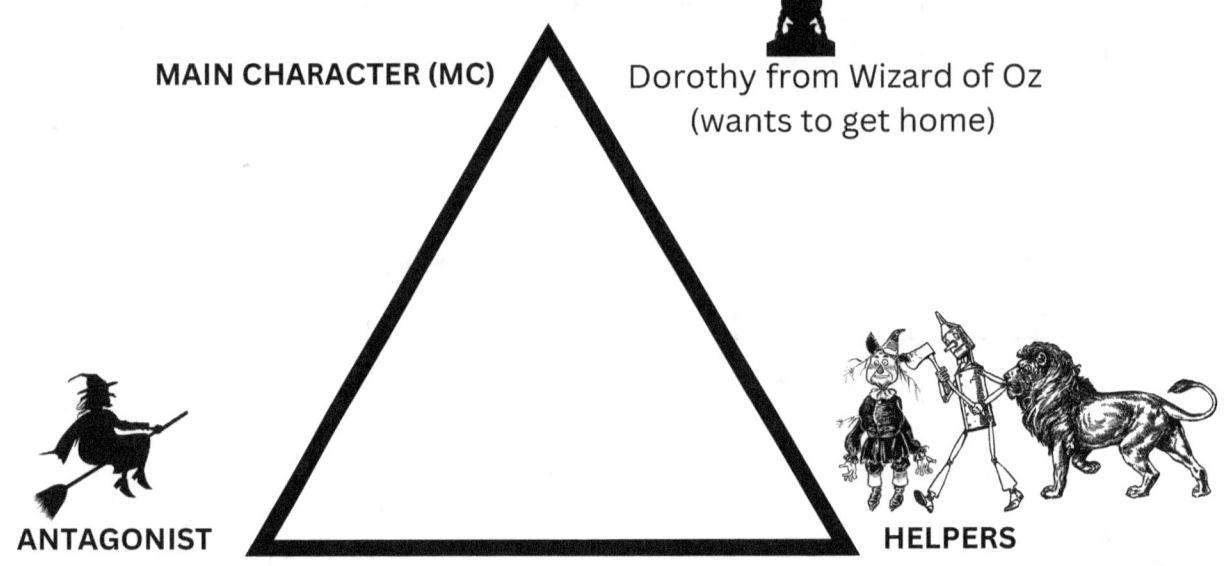

MAIN CHARACTER (MC) Dorothy from Wizard of Oz
(wants to get home)

ANTAGONIST **HELPERS**

Wicked Witch of the West
(wants the ruby slippers)
Q: Is the Wizard an Antagonist for
part of the story?

The Scarecrow (wants a brain)
The Tim Man (wants a heart)
The Lion (wants courage)
The Wizard (wants to go home too)
The Good Witch (wants to defeat WWW)

In more complex stories the Helpers can betray the Main Character and shift alliances catering to their own motives. Each character has a strong desire that can conflict with another character's desire. **Imagine another version of the Wizard of Oz in which the characters have very different motives:**

- The Tin Man could get jealous of the Scarecrow and try to sabotage his relationship with Dorothy.
- The Scarecrow could try to get in the way of Dorothy's motive to go home.
- The Scarecrow could get the Lion to help him make sure she doesn't go.
- Dorothy may not want the Lion to gain courage because as a coward she can control him and he doesn't frighten her. She may try to keep him in line by undermining his self esteem, but in this case she probably would not be the protagonist as main characters are generally sympathetic.

These kinds of conflicts and motives happen in the drama of life with real human beings. Antagonists look different as the stories get closer to reality.

- Sometimes helpers are also antagonists for a time.
- Often the character is their own worst enemy (internal obstacle).

EXAMPLES IN LITERATURE:

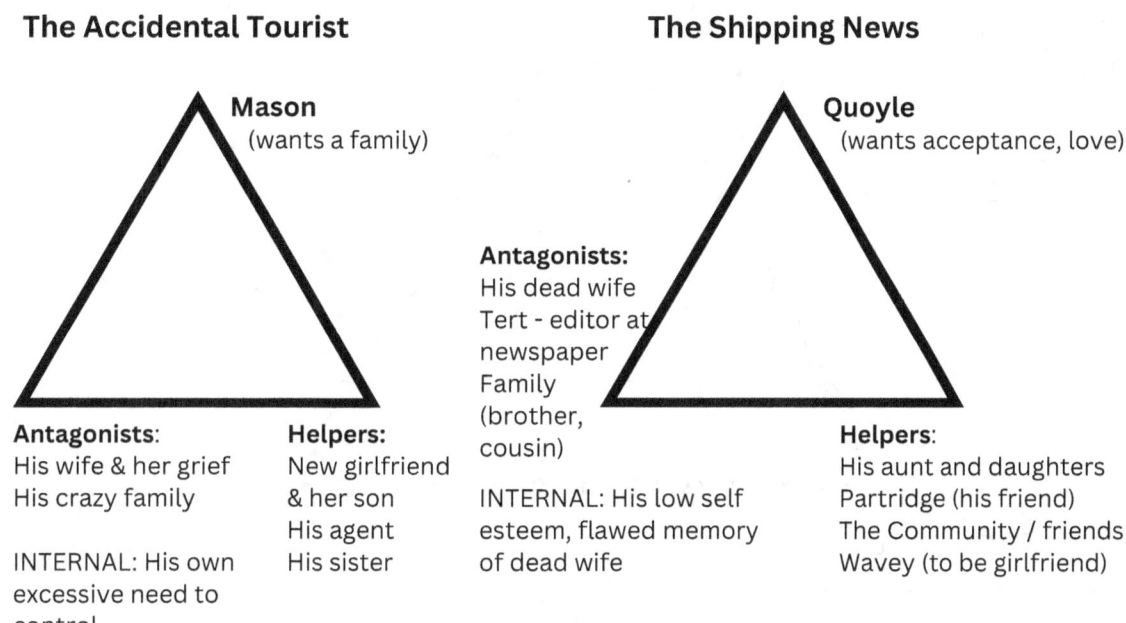

The Accidental Tourist

Mason
(wants a family)

Antagonists:
His wife & her grief
His crazy family

INTERNAL: His own excessive need to control

Helpers:
New girlfriend & her son
His agent
His sister

The Shipping News

Quoyle
(wants acceptance, love)

Antagonists:
His dead wife
Tert - editor at newspaper
Family (brother, cousin)

INTERNAL: His low self esteem, flawed memory of dead wife

Helpers:
His aunt and daughters
Partridge (his friend)
The Community / friends
Wavey (to be girlfriend)

Can you identify the roles in your own story?
Use blanks on next pages to try

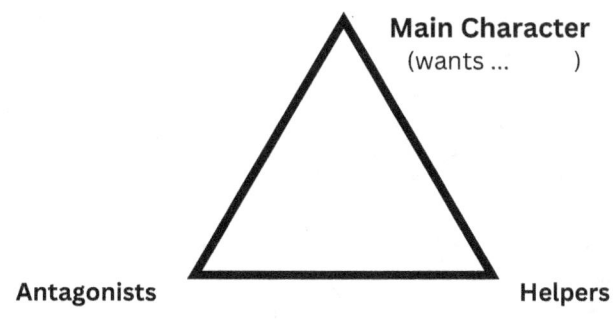

Main Character
(wants ...   )

Antagonists   **Helpers**

INTERNAL:

BLANK Relationship Triangle with Instructions

MAKE UP A TRIANGLE FOR EACH MAJOR CHARACTER IN YOUR STORY

• Put everything you can think that the character might desire inside and around the triangle. Choose the most important one and phrase it in a simple sentence under What they most want.

• List possible Antagonists (people or things that get in the way)

• List possible Helpers (people who can help them defeat their obstacles)

Character: _____ Main Internal Obstacle: _____

What they most want (or trouble they must overcome):

_____

_____

_____

Antagonists

_____
_____
_____
_____
_____
_____
_____
_____
_____
_____

Helpers

_____
_____
_____
_____
_____
_____
_____
_____
_____
_____

Does what each of your characters want differ?

Or do some want the same thing?

How do they become obstacles for each others desires?

How can they help each others desires?

REMEMBER put in at least one obstacle that the character has within them, their **INTERNAL OBSTACLE.**

BLANK Relationship Triangles

Character: _____   **Main Internal Obstacle:** _____

What they most want (or trouble
they must overcome):

_____
_____
_____

Antagonists   **Helpers**

_____   _____
_____   _____
_____   _____
_____   _____
_____   _____
_____   _____
_____   _____
_____   _____

Character: _____   **Main Internal Obstacle:** _____

What they most want (or trouble
they must overcome):

_____
_____
_____

Antagonists   **Helpers**

_____   _____
_____   _____
_____   _____
_____   _____
_____   _____
_____   _____
_____   _____
_____   _____

Character: _____ **Main Internal Obstacle:** _____

What they most want (or trouble
they must overcome):

_____
_____
_____

Antagonists

_____
_____
_____
_____
_____
_____
_____
_____

Helpers

_____
_____
_____
_____
_____
_____
_____
_____

●

Character: _____ **Main Internal Obstacle:** _____

What they most want (or trouble
they must overcome):

_____
_____
_____

Antagonists

_____
_____
_____
_____
_____
_____
_____
_____

Helpers

_____
_____
_____
_____
_____
_____
_____
_____

The 3-Act Paradigm or Story Arc

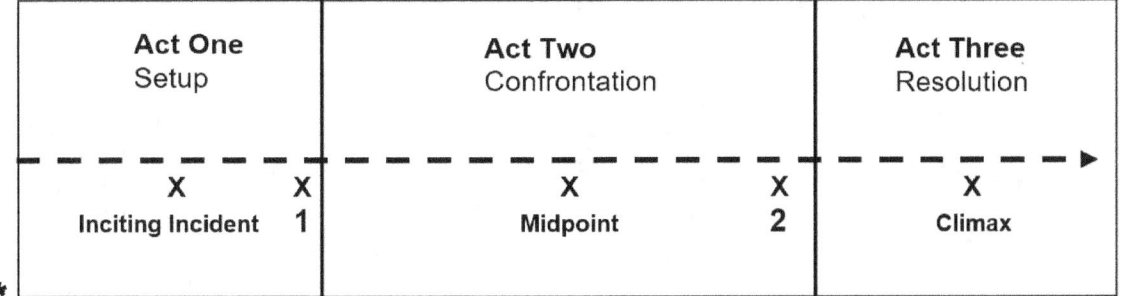

Act One Setup	Act Two Confrontation	Act Three Resolution
X X 1 Inciting Incident	X X 2 Midpoint	X Climax

*

- **Inciting Incident** - something disturbs the norm
- **Plot Point 1** - point of no return - the reluctant hero relents he must go forward
- **Midpoint** - lowest point before battling back
- **Plot Point 2** - the truth is shown, there is some sort of reversal
- **Climax** - maximum tension of opposing forces, chaos goes back to order.

The Hero & Heroine's Journey **

1. Call to Adventure
2. Reluctant Heroine
3. Cross the Threshold
4. Tests, Helpers, Villains
5. Ultimate Ordeal
6. Reward
7. Road back - transformed
8. Triumphant Return

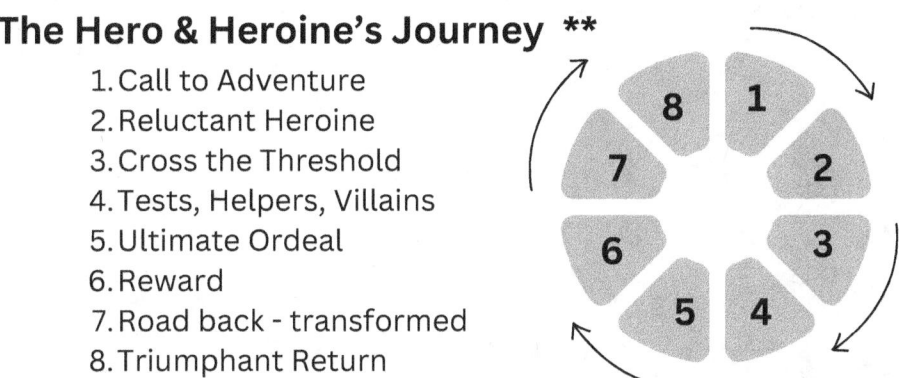

*The first diagram is from the classic 1979 Syd Field's formula for screenplays, used again in *Save the Cat,* and works for novels as well as plays and screenplays. ** *The Heroes Journey* is based on Joseph Campbell's book on myths, later used in Christopher Vogler's *The Writer's Journey,* recommended reading.

Sub plots

The below arc graph confuses most novelists and is perhaps too complex a plotting tool, but some may find it helpful to view for secondary characters' subplots. **KEEP IT SIMPLE**

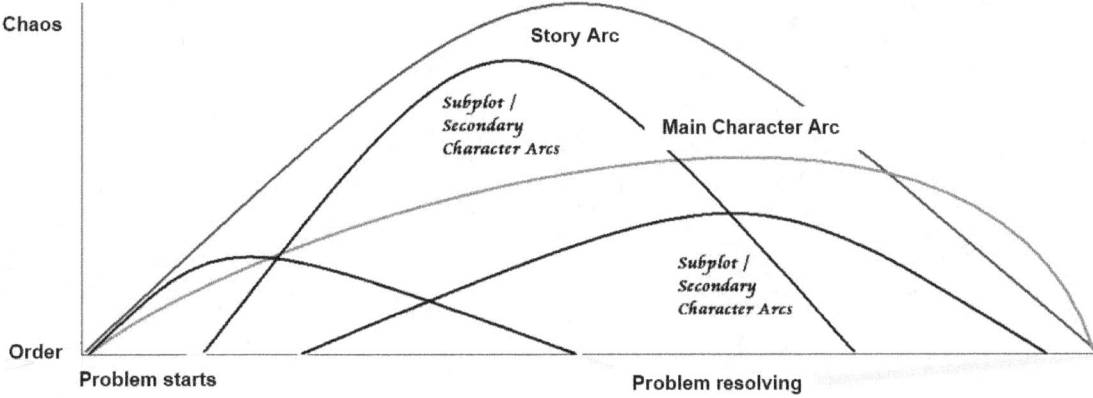

EXAMPLE - Plotting a Novel using 3-Act Structure
Using the *Wizard of Oz* movie as an Example.

The Plot Points	Description	Dangers/ Obstacles / Villains	Character Flaws/Strengths	Notes / Friends / Helpers
Inciting Incident - The thing that propels the story forward.	Toto is taken away from Dorothy	Wicked woman in town, Tornado	Determined, good, head strong, loves people	Meet others: Auntie Em, farm friends, Prof Marvel, Toto
Plot Point One - The Point of No return - a deeper adventure has started	Gets Toto back runs away but caught in the Tornado and lands in Oz killing the wicked witch	The wicked witch of the West wants the ruby slippers and revenge	Kind, accepting, polite, makes friends	Good witch, munchkins
First Challenge that gets in the way of what the character wants is taken on	Starts on Yellow brick road	Wicked witch still plagues her. Friends she meets need help	Kind, accepting, polite, makes friends. Wants to help others	Scarecrow
Second Challenge	Troubles along road including being put to sleep by witch with poppies	Wicked witch still plagues her. Poppies	Kind, accepting, polite, makes friends. Stands up for her friends	Tin Man & Lion add. Good witch helps
Third Challenge	Challenge to get into see the Wizard - He wants witch's broom - Quest	Wiz wants witch's broom. Flying monkeys	Fearful. Working together to overcome fears	Tin man, lion and scarecrow
Plot Point Two - The last Challenge has seemingly defeated them, before it is resolved (by character or by fate)	Dorothy and Toto are taken by the witch	The witch has Dorothy and intends to kill her when hourglass runs out. Getting into castle - the others rescue	The lion overcomes his cowardice. They work together	Tin man, lion, Toto and scarecrow
Plot Point Three or Climax - The character may get what they want but at a potential cost, point of greatest tension before resolution.	They rescue Dorothy, but they are backed into a corner with no way out. They kill the witch accidentally when she lights the scarecrow on fire	The witch. Fire. The whole army	Her love for auntie Em and home	Tin man, lion and scarecrow
Resolution The character has restored things back to order.	They get the broom back to the Wizard and he refuses to help at first until he helps them thanks to her standing up for her friends	Wizard refusal to help at first	Dorothy stands up for her friends	Toto reveals Wiz. Wiz gives friends their wants. Wiz agrees take Dorothy home. Good witch helps her get there

BLANKS x4 - Plotting a Novel using 3-Act Structure

The Plot Points	Description	Dangers/ Obstacles / Villains	Character Flaws/Strengths	Notes / Friends / Helpers
Inciting Incident - The thing that propels the story forward.				
Plot Point One - The Point of No return - a deeper adventure has started				
First Challenge that gets in the way of what the character wants is taken on				
Second Challenge				
Third Challenge NOTE: You can add more challenges, not just three.				
Plot Point Two - The last Challenge has seemingly defeated them, before it is resolved (by character or by fate)				
Plot Point Three or Climax - The character may get what they want but at a potential cost. point of greatest tension before resolution				
Resolution The character has restored things back to order.				

The Plot Points	Description	Dangers / Obstacles / Villains	Character Flaws/Strengths	Notes / Friends / Helpers
Inciting Incident - The thing that propels the story forward.				
Plot Point One - The Point of No return - a deeper adventure has started				
First Challenge that gets in the way of what the character wants is taken on				
Second Challenge				
Third Challenge NOTE: You can add more challenges, not just three.				
Plot Point Two - The last Challenge has seemingly defeated them, before it is resolved (by character or by fate)				
Plot Point Three or Climax - The character may get what they want but at a potential cost, point of greatest tension before resolution				
Resolution The character has restored things back to order.				

The Plot Points	Description	Dangers/ Obstacles / Villains	Character Flaws/Strengths	Notes / Friends / Helpers
Inciting Incident - The thing that propels the story forward.				
Plot Point One - The Point of No return - a deeper adventure has started				
First Challenge that gets in the way of what the character wants is taken on				
Second Challenge				
Third Challenge NOTE: You can add more challenges, not just three.				
Plot Point Two - The last Challenge has seemingly defeated them, before it is resolved (by character or by fate)				
Plot Point Three or Climax - The character may get what they want but at a potential cost. point of greatest tension before resolution				
Resolution The character has restored things back to order.				

The Plot Points	Description	Dangers/ Obstacles / Villains	Character Flaws/Strengths	Notes / Friends / Helpers
Inciting Incident - The thing that propels the story forward.				
Plot Point One - The Point of No return - a deeper adventure has started				
First Challenge that gets in the way of what the character wants is taken on				
Second Challenge				
Third Challenge NOTE: You can add more challenges, not just three				
Plot Point Two - The last Challenge has seemingly defeated them, before it is resolved (by character or by fate)				
Plot Point Three or Climax - The character may get what they want but at a potential cost, point of greatest tension before resolution				
Resolution The character has restored things back to order.				

EXAMPLE - Chapter / Scene Plotting

This example uses **The Wizard of Oz** movie to show you how you can plot each chapter and its scenes. By using broad strokes first to describe the chapter, purpose and climax you will be able to break your novel into scenes later. This can also work for screenplays.

Use the **blank plotting tables in the following pages** to set out your chapters.
NOTE: You may want to copy a blank page first, or recreate in a spreadsheet so you can have more to use and make changes.

Ch. #	Description of Scenes / Chapter	Chapter / Scene Purpose	Climax of Ch / Scn. Point of Greatest Tension
1	We get to know Dorothy, her family, her friends at farm, and Toto her beloved dog. **Inciting Incident:** The wicked woman who hates Toto.	Dorothy vs. Wicked Woman PURPOSE: ARGUE TO SAVE TOTO	Toto is taken away by wicked woman who threatens the sheriff to her aunt and uncle.
2	Toto escapes back to Dorothy and she decides they must run away. Meets Prof. Marvel who persuades her to return home.	She stops running away and starts to return but gets caught in the TORNADO.	Her decision to go home but with impending storm.
3	In house in tornado she sees the wicked woman turn into a witch on a broom. House falls and kills the witch and she finds herself in Oz. Meets munchkins, Wicked Witch of he West and Glinda the Good Witch who gives her the ruby slippers.	She starts quest to Wizard on yellow brick road to get home. START JOURNEY TO GET HOME (Plot Pt. 1 - point of no return)	The wicked witch threatens her and we know her path will be dangerous.

Chapter / Scene Plotting BLANK

Ch. #	Description of Scene(s) / Chapter	Chapter / Scene Purpose	Climax of Chapter

Ch. #	Description of Scene(s) / Chapter	Chapter / Scene Purpose	Climax of Chapter

Ch. #	Description of Scene(s) / Chapter	Chapter / Scene Purpose	Climax of Chapter

Ch. #	Description of Scene(s) / Chapter	Chapter / Scene Purpose	Climax of Chapter

Point-of-View (POV)

Review the three major kinds of POV to use and their attributes correctly. Generally, I tell new writers writing their first long-form fiction project, to stick with the POV they are most comfortable writing in before they try others.

1st person - the "I" main character narrator, often narrates throughout, strictly from their point-of-view. This must remain throughout the whole chapter and usually the whole book. **EXAMPLE:**

> I thought it was funny he should say that. I toyed with the idea of telling him the truth but decided to save it; not today.

3rd person - the POV is limited to narrating only what one character (at a time) would know or see or think, and uses he/she/they pronouns. You should not change character points of view in the same scene or chapter. If it is from the protagonist's point of view at the start of the chapter it remains that throughout the chapter. Their thoughts, when they are speaking to themselves in their head, are written in italics and should be brief one or two line sentences, no more. **EXAMPLE:**

> *Funny he should say that. Should I tell him the truth?* She decided, not today.

Note that in this example above the third person thoughts can use the "I" as in 1st person, but only for a brief sentence or two, and thoughts are in italics.

Omni (omniscient) - the god-like omniscient narrator that knows what is happening all over and every character's thoughts. The narrator uses pronouns (he/she/they) and the characters' own names. When the character's thoughts are revealed it does not require quotation marks any longer, unless they are quoting or creating a slogan or something, and it generally is not in italics, as that suggests 3rd person (although there is some leeway on that one). Generally, the Omni narrator says characters thoughts like this **EXAMPLE:**

> Jane thought it was funny he should say that. While she toyed with the idea of telling him the truth, she didn't notice that Ted was watching her carefully.

Omni narrators can know what is happening in the past and future for all characters at any time, or all at the same time. They can be hidden or obvious, but these days the style is to use a hidden narrator when using Omni. NOTE: a narrator/character who is telling the story in a flashback at the beginning of the story or chapter is technically 3rd person or 1st.

Recommended Reading: Browne and King's *Self Editing for Fiction Writers*.

Chapter / Scene Breaks

While writing your manuscript you may, or may not, be choosing where there is a chapter break and where there needs to be a section break or a line break. These are things you often determine afterward, but it is good to know why you do them and which to use.

The Three Primary Shifts
- **Time**
- **Location**
- **POV**

In any of these three kinds of shifts in the narrative you may want to use a line break, a section break or a chapter break. Which you use is determined by how big the shift is, as well as other creative factors. These can be used in memoirs or any narrative writing.

Small Shift = Line Break

This is a line of white space in the narrative. This is usually a small time shift or a small location shift, or both together. It means a few minutes later, or somewhere else in the vicinity, possibly as much as across town but that would more likely be a scene break, rarely would it suddenly be in a different city. Line breaks are generally too small to connote a POV shift.

Medium Shift = Scene or Section Break

This is a break with three stars in the center of the page along with line spaces. it may be used for any of the three shifts but generally time or location, and not POV.

***

The standard stars may also be creative doo-dads that the publisher chooses.

Big Shift = Chapter Break

A big shift usually calls for a chapter break. Generally, if it is a time shift, and requires more than a section or line break it means, days, months or years have gone by. If a location shift, the main character is in a different location as well as time has past.

Another common reason to take a chapter break is the author is using another point of view, often 3rd person from another character's perspective than what they have been previously using. There are many other creative reasons an author may choose a chapter break, and none better than suspense. The next topic is Open Loops and how to use them in storytelling and especially for chapter breaks.

Open Loops
for Chapter Breaks in Fiction and Memoirs

Have you ever binge watched a series on Netflix? Chances are you hung in there because at the end of each episode there was an Open Loop. In effect open loops are cliff hangers, but not necessarily overly dramatic ones. Something has to be left undone, unresolved, or unanswered in a narrative to create an open loop. The readers' brains will then want to resolve or close it.

For years regular TV shows always had a resolution at the end of the episode, except for soap operas and telenovelas, which usually had something ultra dramatic left hanging… or open. They have very dedicated viewers. Now every TV show is like that and if something resolves, something else has to be unresolved.

Keeping readers turning the pages is often a case of keeping them in some kind of suspense even a subtle one. That is why when **planning your chapter breaks** you should plan an open loop at or near the end of the chapter. If there isn't one, you should find one and change where you had your chapter break, or create one. A reader will keep reading to find out if that intriguing open loop will be closed in the next chapter. And that open loop may go on for more than one chapter, so it does mean that if you resolve it, in the next chapter you will have to open another loop, however subtle, at the end of the chapter, or bring back the previous one with a new twist.

A lack of open loops is as big a problem in Memoirs as in Fiction; it is just not good storytelling. Worse, is that new writers often destroy the suspense by telling the reader what is about to happen, also known as telegraphing.

EXAMPLE:

> "If someone had told me then that he would be the man of my dreams I never would have believed them."

Better would be…

> "I thought this annoying yet handsome man was quite full of himself, and I was glad I wouldn't be seeing him again."

With this statement, readers will suspect that she will be seeing him again and hang on to find out for sure if this is someone important.

Checklist for Fiction Writers

BEFORE WRITING or JUST WRITTEN

☐ Determine Climax and Purpose of the scene or chapter.
Does the chapter build and leave in a new place?

☐ Character scene intention - each scene may change with the
characters specific intention.

☐ Show vs. Tell check. Are you telling or showing?

☐ Story test – can I make the stakes higher?

☐ Character purpose goes throughout whole story (sometimes shifts
with epiphany)

☐ POV check – in 3rd person - only one character at a time possible

AFTER WRITTEN

☐ Flow test – are too many details preventing story from flowing forward

☐ Dialogue Test – say everything out loud in character's voice

☐ Is there enough description and orientation? Ex: Is each character
and location introduced to the reader?

☐ Time shifts – full chapter break or full line break

☐ Location shifts – describe and orient just enough, full chapter break or full
line break

☐ If there is a change in POV then... usually full chapter break or a *** break

☐ Open Loop test - is there one at the end of each chapter?

☐ Telegraphing check - destroying suspense - Are you giving it away OR
allowing suspense?

☐ Evil Puppet Master test – Am I listening to my character? What clues?
(from *Writing with Cold Feet)*

☐ Plot holes and Plausibility check – Is this a realistic scenario? What's
missing to make this plausible? Would this likely happen in reality? In your
fantasy world?

☐ Continuity check, did we forget something for continuity? Did color of hair
or eyes change on the same character? Beta readers catch these often.

☐ Final POV checking – Did you switch POVs in the middle of a chapter or
scene with no proper break. Editors and beta readers also catch this.

Timeline Example found in MS Word SMART Art

When doing research for a longform narrative you may need to make a timeline. In MS Word you can find a template under the **INSERT tab > SmartArt and scroll down to find under Process heading, choose the one called Basic Timeline.** It is simple and obvious to use remember to add dates as well as text.

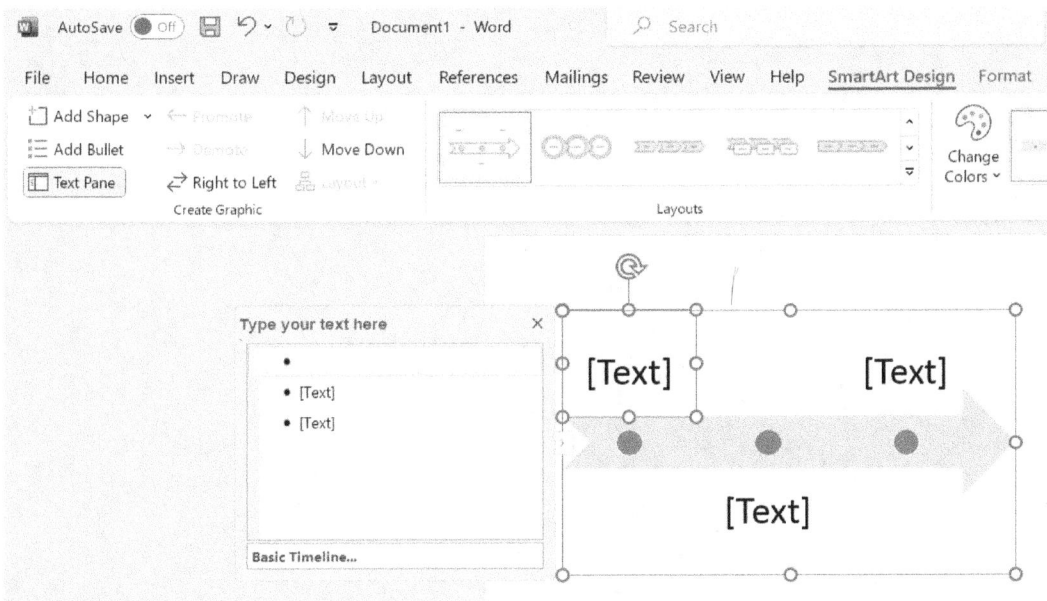

Result looks like this:

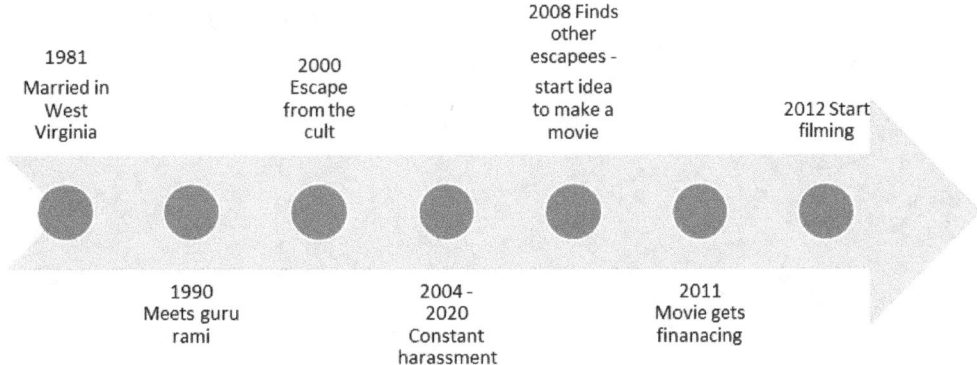

Plotting out your characters or your stories timeline as it happens in history helps keep you clear.

FOR

Nonfiction Writers

(writers of memoirs, biographies, self help books, etc.)

Framework for Self Help Book Structure

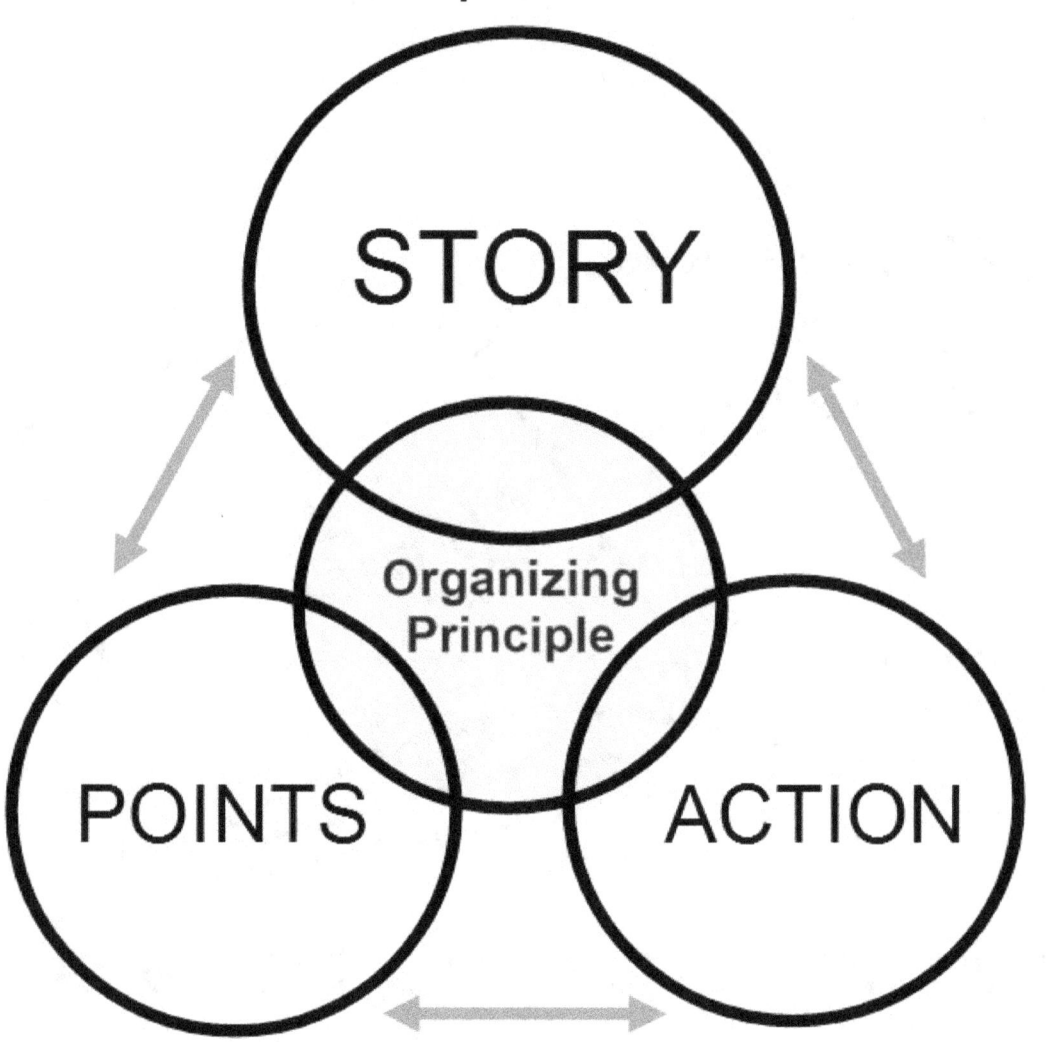

An Organizing Principle is often seen in Successful Self Help Titles

Titles	The Organizing Principle
The Four Agreements	(# of Agreements)
The Seven Habits of Highly Effective People	(# of Habits)
Men are from Mars, Women are from Venus	(Compare men and women)
The Secrets of How to Write	(Secrets)
The Myths and Lies of Marriage	(Myths and Lies)
The 17 Day Diet	(# of Days)

Other Examples of Organizing Principles

(and title of book)

- Principles
- Tips
- Stories (*Chicken Soup* - Stories for ...)
- Meditations
- Steps
- Arguments
- Paths
- Keys
- Seasons
- Alphabet (ex. my book: The *A to Zen of Writing*)
- Question and Answer (question often in the title)
- Confessions
- Secrets
- Lies
- Choices

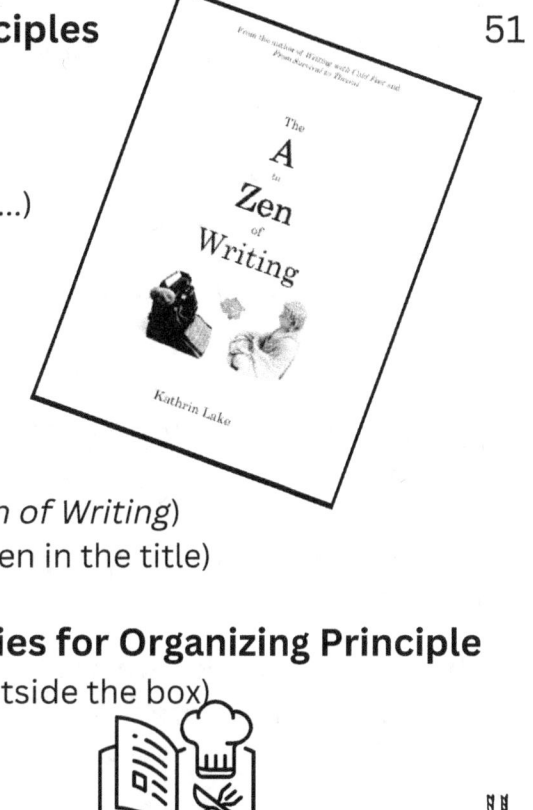

Other Possibilities for Organizing Principle

(these are more outside the box)

- Food – recipes
- Photos
- Then and Now
- Compare and Contrast
- An Object - doors, cups
- Geography - here and there
- Fantasy & Reality
- Knots
- Floors in a Building

ADD IN:

- Tie to subject
- Who the book is for &/or talking about
- The thesis or theme
- A framework (a diagram that models the central idea in the book)
- Locations
- Situations
- A number

Getting Clear on the Subject - Self Help Title Brainstorm Questions
Write your answers before starting (or finishing) your book

What is the main problem you solve or solution you provide? What is your expertise? (Is it Googlable? Blatant? Human interest?)

What's the best and most impactful service you provide to the world, or message you really want to share?

Who needs your help? What type of people? What do they do? Who specifically?

What unique problem(s) does who you are helping have? What do they want?

What opportunities are possible for these people that they are not aware of, but you are?
(FICTION WRITERS: What does your main character want?)

What challenges would exist if you did not have the knowledge, skills, products and expertise you have now? And what challenges exist for these people without your expertise?
FICTION WRITERS: What's in the way of your character getting what he/she wants?

What successes have you had because of your knowledge, skills, products and expertise?
FICTION WRITERS: Does your character succeed or fail? What does he/she learn by trying to succeed, or what does he/she get that may be even better?

What successes have your clients had because of your help?

How do I present the way I will help so it is graspable to others (organizing principle)**?**

How fast or easily can a person do this to solve their problem? 21 days, 10 easy steps? (if applicable)

_____

_____

_____

_____

_____

_____

_____

_____

_____

_____

_____

You can use organizing principles used before or think outside the box:
Habits ...   Elevator Floors...
Agreements ...   Meal Courses

Title:

_____

What is the organizing principle? Is it in the title or subtitle? Is there a poetry to it, or double-take words in it? Ex: *Who moved my cheese?*

Subtitle:

_____

_____

BE MORE SPECIFIC: Who is the book for? What result does it promise? What problem does it solve? What is it about? How do you say it to the uninitiated so they understand? How do you make it clear but catchy? Is it a series?

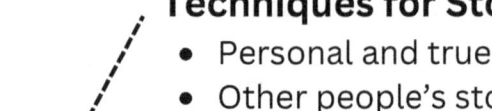

Techniques for Story

- Personal and true stories
- Other people's stories
- Stories of the famous and successful
- Dialogue
- Case Studies
- Metaphors – to make a parallel
- Anecdotes – short stories for a point
- Examples –short stories w no beginnings
- Myths (Historical, Fairytales)

STORY

Organizing Principle

POINTS

ACTION

Techniques for Points

The NATURAL POINT(s) that come from each story

Back up the points with:
- Quotes
- Facts & Stats
- Studies
- Benefits
- Suppositions or Hypotheticals
- Q&A
- A Rhetorical Question (obvious answer)

Techniques for Action

- Homework
- Call to action
- Reflection
- Fill ins
- Lists
- Questions
- Reader fills in Answers
- Their Creation (homework assignment)
- Prescriptions
- Events
- Field Trip
- Research
- Note: Workbooks are mostly action

The Simple Structure for your Self Help Book

EXAMPLE: Organizing Principle is: **Secrets**
"The Three Secrets to Successful Dating"
For singles who are fed up with dating apps

1. Introduction

2. Secret one ⎤
   a. Story ⎥ The Secrets can be sections
   b. Points ⎦ or chapters. See example
   c. Action   below of sections
a. Story
b. Points
c. Action
   a. Story
   b. Points
   c. Action
Sum up chapter/section and actions
Set ground for next chapter/section

3. Secret two
   a. Points
   b. Story
   c. Action
a. Story
b. Points
c. Action
   a. Story
   b. Points
   c. Action
Sum up chapter/section and actions
Set ground for next chapter/section

4. Secret three
   a. Points ⎤ **Note**: You can
   b. Story ⎥ change the
   c. Action ⎥ order and start
a. Story ⎥ with the points
b. Points ⎦ (or actions)
c. Action
   a. Story
   b. Points
   c. Action
Sum up chapter/section and actions. Set ground for next chapter/section

5. Conclusion
Sum up entire book reviewing all

Note: Your book may have less or more than three stories in each chapter or section. Sections were used in my book *Writing with Cold Feet,* with chapters in each section. See lay out in Contents below with 5 sections of secrets.

TITLE:
Writing with Cold Feet
SUBTITLE:
Secrets of How to Write When You Are NOT Writing

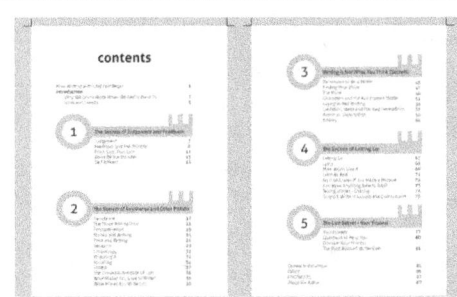

Note: See also the basic order of pages for publishing at the end of this workbook.

Plotting Worksheets for Nonfiction
Rough out your chapters using these tables

Chapter # & Brief description	Major Theme or Purpose	List the sub points in the chapter	Intro to Chapter subject (try to keep intro style somewhat consistent for each chapter)	Point 1 Story, example, metaphor or case study. What is the sub point that it supports?	Point 2 Story, example, metaphor or case study. What is the sub point that it supports?	Point 3 Story, example, metaphor or case study. What is the sub point that it supports?	Chapter Conclusion List Actions or reflections that you want from reader?

Rough out your chapters using these tables

Non-Fiction Structure (how-to or self-help books)

Working Title and Subtitle of Book (use as overarching guide of the purpose)
REMINDER: Titles are a Promise to the Reader

Chapter # & Brief description	Major Theme or Purpose	List the sub points in the chapter	Intro to Chapter subject (try to keep intro style somewhat consistent for each chapter)	Point 1 Story, example, metaphor or case study. What is the sub point that it supports?	Point 2 Story, example, metaphor or case study. What is the sub point that it supports?	Point 3 Story, example, metaphor or case study. What is the sub point that it supports?	Chapter Conclusion List Actions or reflections that you want from reader?

Memoirs

What is the difference between an **autobiography** and a **memoir**?

Autobiographies

- Cradle to late life story
- Often covers parents
- Covers all life highlights
- Chronological
- Tends to be a recounting versus creative
- Often celebrities

Memoirs

- Has a focus
- Has a theme or message
- Starts and ends at ANY relevant period of the person's life according to the focus
- Is not necessarily told chronologically
- Tends to be more creative nonfiction

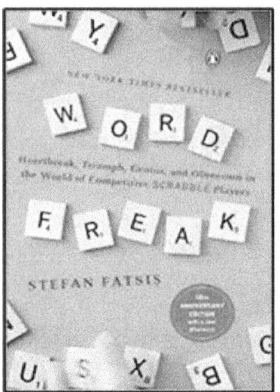

Memoirs have a focus. This one is about Scrabble and the author's experience in Scrabble tournaments, and interviewing champions.

The following worksheets come from this book on writing Memoirs with permission.

Memoir Planning - Questionnaire

What is your message or focus of your memoir?
One word or phrase: _____
The opposite of above (you can use it to add contrast in your story):
_____

Over how many years (or days) does this take place? Years-Dates:
_____

Does it have one timeline or more than one (flashbacks)? Explain them:
_____
_____

How did you (the main character) change?
_____

What is the through-line of this story? Finish these prompts...
    This is the story of a woman/man who...
    And overcame...
    To...
    Along the way they...

Who helped you?
_____

Who did the opposite? _____

What are the centerpiece stories? (crucial incidents, revelations or turning points)
1) _____
2) _____
3) _____
4) _____

Visuals to add: Photos, Graphics, Drawings, etc.
_____

What is the Historical Backdrop at this time? _____
_____

Does history play a part in your story? How? _____
_____

Memoir Do's and Don'ts

1. **Don't** try to write it chronologically. Start with what you do remember and write the moment that attracts you first and then you can right the beginning later.
2. **Do** just write, and keep writing.
3. **Don't** tone it down. Be honest and fearless.
4. **Do** go with your emotions, be they positive or negative. Write from your heart because that is where the story is.
5. Part way through, **Do** look for an organizing theme (or themes) which may emerge, to give yourself a structure (ex: *A Year in Provence* starts with seasons). Others are divided into messages or themes. My memoir, The Happy Hammock, has many themes but the one that I tried to bring out was community. You may have your own theme deep in the background and no one else can see it but it supports you.
6. **Don't** think about publishing or sharing your story yet. It could close you down.
7. **Do** journal and always keep it handy when stories and memories come back to you. (See Story Log).
8. **Do** write for yourself or for someone you are excited to tell the story to, but remember that there's always time to go back and make it clearer for others later, that's called editing and you will get help with that.
9. **Do** ask others for recollections or interview them. It's up to you if you want to interview people from your past or just play it by memory. If you decide to do interviews, just remember that no one's memory is going to be perfect. Some folks might not even remember things that you remember, because their focus was elsewhere or they have long since forgotten, or they focus on themselves. Everyone sees even the same event differently but their picture might make a better story. Your choice.
10. **Do** use photos and objects to jog memories.
11. **Do** make up or imagine the bits that are details and transitions that no one knows and no one can refute, in order to tell a better story. This is the most important point: no one loves a storyteller for their accuracy. **Don't** try to write it 100% accurate, instead, make a good story.
12. **Do** understand fictional storytelling form so that you know what makes a good story. Recommended reading: *How to Write an Enthralling Memoir Using Fiction Techniques*.
13. **Do** try to write as if it were happening in the present, as much as possible.
14. **Do** include dialogue (even if you are making some of it up). Dialogue Test – read everything out loud in person's voice. It should sound natural and flow.

Interviewing Techniques

If you want to interview people from your past here are some techniques to help you.

- Use memory jogs - photos, videos, clothes and objects.
- Who are the most critical people to interview? List them.
- Try to bring up a specific, emotional or dramatic memory to ask about.
- Listen - you will learn more by not pressing one agenda.
- Prompting questions: Who, How, Why, What did you/they say?
- Tell your version and let them fill in the gaps. Or add theirs.

Timelining* Significant Incidents

List significant events for your memoir and reflect on their meaning. And pay attention to any turning points. Timelining significant incidents ahead may also allow you to decide if some parts of the story should be told non-chronologically. Many memoirs start with a turning point and then go back to how you got there. You may need a separate page and this will often change before you get it right.
*Note: page 47 shows you how to do a Timeline in MS Word that may be valuable.

Start Year_____
Date_____
_____
_____

Significant Incident_____
_____
Year_____
_____
_____

Significant Incident_____
_____
Year_____
_____
_____

Significant Incident_____
_____
Year_____
_____
_____

Significant Incident_____
_____
Year_____
_____
_____

Turning Point_____
_____

Significant Incident_____
_____
Year_____
_____
_____

Significant Incident_____
_____
Year_____
_____
_____

Turning Point_____
_____

Significant Incident_____
_____
Year_____
_____

Turning Point_____
Revelation_____
_____
Year_____
Closing Incident_____
_____
Year End_____

Story Logging for Memoirs (and other Nonfiction)

We need stories. We want stories. We tell stories constantly. But we sometimes forget some of them, until something or someone reminds us. This is why you should start story logging. I make notes on my phone constantly, but I used to use paper and even write on my hand when reminded of a good story in my life I didn't want to forget to document later. These are the stories we bring out at dinner and cocktail parties that you need to capture. When I make a note of one, I transfer the reminder of it to a simple log like the one below.

Examples :			
STORY	POINT / LESSON	REFECTION/ACTION	THEME
First Kiss	Desire greater than fear	Vulnerability	Innocence
Nearly drowned when 10	Sometimes you take risks	Mum sometimes knows	Rebelling
Rescued brother	Blood is thick	Remember connections	Protection of Family

It is great to be able to determine the points and lessons and also give it a theme. Then it is easy to retrieve multiple suitable stories when you find you are trying to make a point, teach a lesson or write to a theme.

Collecting these stories is not only important for memoirists, but nonfiction authors and experts in any field. This is especially important for speakers, trainers and presenters (ex: TED talk speakers).

Story Log - Blank

STORY	POINT / LESSON	REFECTION/ACTION	THEME

Story Log - Blank

STORY	POINT / LESSON	REFECTION/ACTION	THEME

Writing Depth and Style - Rewriting!

Famous writers have said, rightly, that all real writing is rewriting. But what should you look at in rewriting your drafts? Two things: Depth and Showing (vs. telling) The below comparisons should help you understand.

Draft 1:

My father was always hard on me. From earliest childhood, I knew this was what to expect. It was almost a family tradition.

Draft 5:

I would come to know that patriarchal discipline was ingrained into the very fabric of the family. It had gone on for generations and didn't break for holidays, births, funerals or world wars. It always got transmitted in torturous exactness from father to son to son — and even to sons-in-law- (by some osmotic process) as men married into the family. None of the children could escape, and this oppressive mantle was now being passed to me.

NOTE: The above examples are both TELL and NOT SHOW.

However, the latter draft 5 is much more evocative. To tell the stories effectively in this memoir, this writer will have to start showing, and thus, bringing memories and stories to life using fiction techniques as I recommend.

In example:

TELL would be:

He was an intimidating man.

SHOW:

He gave me a glare that was so penetrating with disapproval that it was impossible for any ordinary human, let alone a youngster, to hold his gaze. The tone of his voice seemed controlled and even, but the pitch of it contained an edge that betrayed rage beneath.

NOTES: The above is not written in the present tense, yet it makes a reader feel as if they are in the moment, being stared down. The sense of sound is evoked from the mention of tone of voice. Using any of the five senses is critical. This is show vs. tell.

Story Types / Themes (Fiction and Non-Fiction)

There are many classic story types, and it can be useful to make your story stronger to know what types or themes you may have in your story, and what emotions you may be triggering.

1. Tragedy to Triumph
2. Dark Horse – unlikely hero
3. Cinderella (rags to riches)
4. Serendipity (happy accident or finding)
5. David vs. Goliath
6. The Aha! Eureka solution
7. The Tough Choice – do the right thing
8. Resolve the Past
9. Move from Victim to Responsible
10. Self Absorbed to Service
11. The Surprise or Prank (humor)
12. The Family dynamic (dark or happy ending)
13. The Humbling
14. The Shaming
15. Becoming a Mentor or being mentored
16. The Stranger
17. Free at Last
18. The Protest
19. The Quest
20. The Tragedy that could have been averted
21. Humans are all the same
22. The *Do It Anyways* (despite told not to) or *Just Watch Me* or the *Prove It!*
23. The Moment of Magic – there is more to earth than you dreamed of
24. Against the Grain or Road Less Travelled (doing the opposite)
25. The Stubborn Persistence
26. The Nostalgia with reflection
27. The Cautionary Tale or Moral
28. The Turning Point
29. The Misdirection - Surprise
30. The Regret - Missed Opportunity
31. The Miracle
32. The Secret Revealed
33. The Above and Beyond
34. The Red Face (embarrassment)
35. Sheer Faith
36. The Complex Solution
37. If you can't beat them, join them
38. Ironic ending
39. The Deep Reflection
40. The Finding of True Self - Authenticity

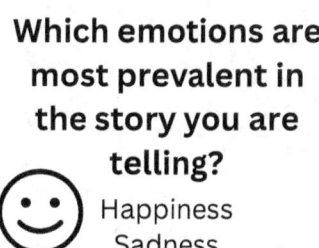

Which emotions are most prevalent in the story you are telling?

Happiness
Sadness
Anger
Surprise
Fear
Disgust
Shame

Fiction + Non-Fiction = Creative Non-Fiction

What makes **Fiction** fiction, and **Nonfiction** non-fiction? And, what is this thing called **Creative Nonfiction**? The images below are how they teach kids the difference between fiction and nonfiction. The lists below go further and show how we can define fiction, nonfiction and creative nonfiction, and the techniques are used for each.

▲ How they teach kids ▲

Fiction +	Non-Fiction =	Creative Nonfiction
Characters	Real or True (*What's that?*)	Real people
Created	Facts	Reality with Creative perspective
Narrative (Story)	Informative over Narrative	Often Narrative
Setting	Educational or Issue-based	Can inform
Descriptive	Can have Arguments (Thesis)	Message/Moral
Message/Moral	Points / Messages / Lessons	Theme
Theme	Subject	Theme

Techniques	Techniques	Techniques
Char. Development	Told by an Authority/Reporter	Real Characters
Story Development	Arguments, Points, Comparisons	Story (Through-line)
Dialogue	Quotes of experts	Dialogue
Setting/World Creation	Rhetoric	Setting
Descriptive prose	Research references	Descriptive prose of reality
Pacing	Structured or Ordered	Narrative or loosely structured
Point of view (multiple)	Neutral or (1st person authority)	Generally 1st person

Examples	Examples	Examples
Novels	Articles	Personal essay
Short Stories	News Stories	Editorial
Novellas	Report	Literary journalism
Children's stories	Essay	Lyric essay/ Blog
Plays	Autobiography	Memoir
Screenplays	Documentary	Docudrama
Poetry	Self-Help / How To	Unclassifiable prose
Flash Fiction	History blurbs	Non-Fiction novella
Graphic Novels	Guide Books / Manuals	Creative Guidebook
Based on True Story	Obituary /Biography	Eulogy / Based on True Life

Basic Order of Pages for Publishing

Front Cover
Title
Subtitle
Author
One Prime Endorsement from good source: "From the Author of…", etc.
Awards

Back Cover
Brief Synopsis - selling it, intriguing, enticement to read
Bullet points
Endorsement blurbs (recommended)
Very brief bio of Author (optional)
Photo of author (optional)
UPC code with ISBN (code and # is mandatory, but adding a price is optional)

Interior
(R=starts on right side page, L= found often on left side page)
(R&L) Advance Praise (optional)
(R) Title Page
(L) Copyright Page
(R) Dedication and/or Acknowledgments and/or Other titles by the same Author (optional)
(R) Table of Contents (nonfiction)
(R) Foreword (nonfiction, optional), written by someone else recognizable
(R) Preface (nonfiction, optional)
(R) Introduction (nonfiction)
(R) Prologue (fiction, optional)
(R) Chapter Headings (fiction and nonfiction)
(R) Endnotes (nonfiction, optional)
(R) Index &/or Glossary &/or Appendix in that order (non-fiction, optional)
(R or L) About the Author bio and photo
(R or L) Marketing for other books and cover photos

About the Author

When Kathrin was eight, she make up stories, cast other kids in parts, raided her mother's closet and then started rehearsals immediately. Much later she studied theatre and film at Simon Fraser University in Vancouver, B.C., Canada. Although she developed a passion for nonfiction by writing for newspapers and other publications, it was being in Theatre that reignited her storytelling days as a child. She collaborated with award-winning Canadian playwrights and even formed a brief writing partnership with the late, great comedy writer, Irwin Barker. She even started winning some awards and prizes herself in playwriting and screenplay writing. On a dare, she started a newspaper in Vancouver called *The Drive* in the happening arts area.

Later, Kathrin cofounded The Vancouver School of Writing and is a fulltime writer, story coach and professional speaker. Her first nonfiction book was *From Survival to Thrival*, but her most popular book is *Writing with Cold Feet*. She has also written *The A to Zen of Writing* and *The Happy Hammock* memoir series. In fiction, she writes murder mysteries under the pseudonym, Kate Lovecraft.

http://kathrinlake.com
http://buddhapress.com
http://vancouverschoolofwriting.com

Other books you may like to read by this author:

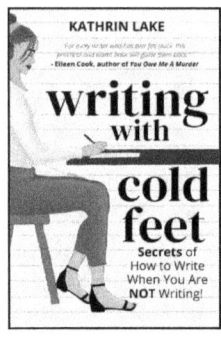

www.ingramcontent.com/pod-product-compliance
Lightning Source LLC
Chambersburg PA
CBHW080339290526
45790CB00010B/3756